MY WONDER LINE

WRITTEN BY
VICKY GOODEN

ILLUSTRATED BY
ANGELA MAYERS

www.bunbunbooks.co.uk

First published in the United Kingdom by Bun Bun Books 2021

Text copyright © Vicky Gooden 2020
Illustrations copyright © Angela Mayers 2020

All rights reserved. No part of this book may be reproduced or transmitted in any form or by any means whatsoever without express written permission from the author, except in the case of brief quotations embodied in critical articles and reviews.

The moral rights of the author and illustrator have been asserted.

ISBN 978-1-5272-7437-2

Printed in the United Kingdom using FSC certified paper.

A CIP catalogue record for this book is available from the British Library.

www.mywonderline.com

For Elodie Willow, our little lion heart...

To the girl with sweet curls and a head full of song.
You have shown what it truly means to be strong.
Your heart is a home to all things sunny and my heart is all yours,
always will be, love Mummy x
- V.G

For Kieran. Thank you for all your love, support
and endless cups of tea, love Angie Doll x
- A.M

Morning awakes and our eyes open wide.
A knock at the door - let's greet who's behind.
Pull back the curtains - the day has begun.
Trees wave their leaves, blinking droplets of sun.

Outside trotting by you could spot a dog,
Or a bushy grey squirrel mid-leap on a log.
From a window up high peeks a kitten or two.
On top of the table is breakfast for you.

So many things that we search for and see... but look, wait a minute...

... there is me.

There's a line between my belly and chin.
But why is it there?

Let me begin...

When you were younger, a friendly nurse said,
"Come take a nap on this hospital bed."

Then it was time for your dreams to begin as doctors
and nurses fixed something within.

While doctors were there behind your line,
they fixed what was broken, taking their time.

They scattered some magic and watered it in,
And that's why you now have a mark on your skin.

Behind my line, is there a door?
Or maybe a hole to jump down and explore?
Is there a room with a track and a train that loops up and down
and then back round again?
Are there balloons that spell out a word?

Tubs of kindness, love and songs, so I've heard.

Are all lines the same, though? What about Mo's?

Mo doesn't have one, that's just how it goes.
Others, like Pearl, have lines different to you.
Each one tells a story, each one something new.
Pearl has a line low down on her tummy…

...It took some getting used to - I thought it looked funny.
I call it my "tum scar" - here, want to see?

If you squint and look this way
it's a branch of a tree.

I sometimes feel different from my friend Belle.
She doesn't have lines, from what I can tell...

But we are all different - just look around.
Some hair spikes up and others curls round.
We can all find something, a part not quite the same.
But imagine a life if we all had the same name!

We'd be topsy and turvy. We'd feel rather upside down.
It's in our different bits where our real stories can be found.

Here comes Belle's brother - his name is Ted.
When he was small, something fell on his head.

He'll tell you about it - he thinks he's real cool.
He shows all the kids in the canteen at school.

You see, my sweet one, this is the truth:

Your line is just part of the WONDERFUL you.

It won't stop you climbing or dancing in shows.
It could help you spread courage wherever you go.

For one day you could meet a new girl or boy
Who has their own line and is lacking in joy.

But you'll know the magic
that lies underneath.

So you can sing...

You could share stories of why your line's there

While queuing for ice creams to slurp at the fair.

See, inside our bodies are feelings and thoughts.
They swirl round and round and sometimes get caught.

But in talking about them,
they move up and on

Which makes us feel lighter until
they feel...gone.

So wrap arms around friends, look up at the sky.
Don't miss those twinkling stars shooting by.

Sit on a hillside, go pick a pear.
Cartwheel, tumble, fly kites through the air!

Just remember -
Your line shows the power deep within you.

Yet there's more that beams through
in the things you do too.

The way that we dress or what makes us giggle -
These too are the things that make us individual.

You have shown strength, such bravery and might.
You are perfectly you, and let's not lose sight

That there's magic inside you, so maybe it's time
That we think of that mark as your...

Wowee! I'm a WONDER! Well, what do you know?
My line marks a story that's mine, mine alone.

I love you sweet one and I'm proud of you so.

Time for a story. Which one would you like?

The one where the boy gets a shiny new bike?

I think what I'd like, just one more time,
Is the story of me and MY WONDER LINE.

ABOUT THE AUTHOR

Vicky Gooden lives in Hertfordshire, UK with her husband and their little one.

Vicky's daughter underwent heart surgery at just over a year old and is the inspiration behind her first book 'My Wonder Line' which she hopes will support other children in finding themselves represented on bookshop shelves.

Vicky is great at getting lost on walks in the woods, rubbing dogs tummies and loves nothing more than bright, chilly days spent in nature with her small person before a stop on the way home for hot chocolate.

Vicky believes that seeing life through a child's eyes is nothing short of magical and has plans to write more children's books.

She is probably busy scribbling down a list of ideas somewhere...